A Big Bike

by Jacob Lee
illustrated by Holly Boyd

Decodable 24

McGraw Hill Education

Bothell, WA • Chicago, IL • Columbus, OH • New York, NY

MHEonline.com

Send all inquiries to:
McGraw-Hill Education
8787 Orion Place
Columbus, OH 43240

ISBN: 978-0-02-138075-6
MHID: 0-02-138075-9

Printed in the United States of America.

7 8 9 LCR 25 24 23

A Girl and a Bike

Hope is on a big red bike.

The girl in red is Rose.
Rose rides with Hope a lot.

Look at Ron.

Can Ron ride?

"You can go with us," Hope told Ron.

A Fun Ride

"Look, you can ride, Ron," smiled Hope.

The bike went up and down big ramps.

Up and down was fun.
Ron and Rose had fun.
Hope was glad.